Urban Farming

HANS & NUNO CLAUZING

AERIAL MEDIA COMPANY

www.clauzingfotografie.nl
www.aerialmediacom.nl
www.facebook.com/Aerialmediacompany

ISBN 978-94-026-0072-8
NUR 424

© 2015 Text copyright: Hans and Nuno Clauzing
© 2015 Illustrations copyright: Hans and Nuno Clauzing
© 2015 First published in hardback by Aerial Media Company, Tiel, The Netherlands

Translation: Marion Coonen-Singor
Editing: Jude Irwin
Cover design and layout: Teo van Gerwen

Aerial Media Company bv.
Postbus 6088
4000 HB Tiel, The Netherlands

Content

5 **Dabbling on public land Battery**

8 **Urban Farm**
New York (United States)

15 **Munthof**
Antwerp (Belgium)

20 **The Biospheric Project Salford, Greater Manchester**
(United Kingdom)

28 **Boeretuin**
Haarlem (The Netherlands)

37 **Edgemere Farm**
New York (United States)

45 **Texelhof**
Haarlem (The Netherlands)

52 **East New York Farms**
New York (United States)

59 **Eagle Street Rooftop Farm**
New York (United States)

65 **Feedback Farms**
New York (United States)

70 **The 462 Halsey community garden**
New York (United States)

77 **Hell's Kitchen Farm Project**
New York (United States)

83 **The Harlem Success Garden**
New York (United States)

89 **North Brooklyn Farms**
New York (United States)

94 **The Riverpark Farm**
New York (United States)

102 **Randall's Island Urban Farm**
New York (United States)

111 **Margarethaland**
The Hague (The Netherlands)

119 **The Youth Farm**
New York (United States)

125 **Dakmoestuin**
Gent (Belgium)

131 **The Site**
Gent (Belgium)

141 **Growing Communities**
London (United Kingdom)

153 **Mobiele moestuin**
Haarlem (The Netherlands)

160 **Rotterdamse Munt**
Rotterdam (The Netherlands)

169 **Het Seinwezen**
Haarlem (The Netherlands)

175 **Torentuin**
Zaltbommel (The Netherlands)

182 **Tuin op de Pier**
Delfshaven Rotterdam (The Netherlands)

DABBLING ON PUBLIC LAND

Actually, I do not particularly like the terms 'urban farming' or 'urban agriculture'. They lead to misunderstandings. The new green wave unleashed by enthusiasts of all sorts in the past decade to transform undeveloped or ugly pieces of land and rooftops into green oases often means so much more than the terms imply. The starting point is always a piece of unused land: messy, neglected plots that have seen better days or are awaiting development – and that's never going to happen because of the economic crisis. Municipalities no longer have the resources or will to tackle this kind of overlooked space, let alone do anything innovative with them. Nor do large-scale, strongly entrenched boroughs that outsource land management to green companies have time for insubordination from citizens.

Sometimes such projects are indeed exclusively about growing food, and have noble ideals and life-enhancing visions behind them. But more often there is a commercial interest involved: restaurant owners, caterers and other creative people suddenly see something in the idea of growing special vegetables, edible flowers and hops for themselves, instead of relying on the choices provided by wholesalers. However, these projects can also help develop city ecologies and make cities attractive for wild flora and fauna. They can give children more natural, educational and adventurous environments in which to play. Or they can create what are known as 'caring gardens'. More and more, urban farming is about making public spaces more beautiful and different, with citizens using their own ideas and not depending on those of planners and officials.

This is how the Toren Tuin (Tower Garden) in Zaltbommel was developed. Together with a group of local residents we adopted a neglected plot of land inside the Zaltbommel fortress, outlined an overall spatial plan and – ignoring both our lack of money and the administrative obstacles – got started. Two seasons and many prizes later, people are still enthusiastic about the place, which is both beautiful and highly valued. Park? Kitchen garden? Flower garden? Bee garden? Natural playground? Orchard? The Tower Garden has it all, but it is first and foremost a human zoo – a green and accessible meeting place made by everyone for everyone.

As a designer, I cannot stress enough how important it is to start with a good spatial plan and a strong vision/concept. This provides a framework for participants and clarity for municipalities, residents and potential sponsors. The best approach is to design a spatial structure that literally gives space to all the green ideas and enthusiasms of many different people, whether or not they have green fingers, and which makes all this beauty accessible to everyone.

Our photographers, Hans and his son Nuno, have taken beautiful photographs of many successful projects both at home and abroad. They were – coincidentally – also guests at the Tower Garden, and were inspired by the enthusiasm of the volunteers and visitors. This same enthusiasm radiates from all the photos in this book.

This amazing book is a tribute to all those people who have the courage to dig and keep digging on public land. I hope it will inspire many new initiatives and provide policymakers with new insights. It is not easy for governments to relinquish control over their public spaces, and initiators often experience negative reactions from their cities at first. This is unfortunate, because I am convinced that this kind of collaboration between citizens and governments can contribute to a new, better, greener interpretation of the public good. Hopefully this book, in which you will be able to see a large number of very successful examples, will contribute to the development and appreciation of the green power of citizens' initiatives. To readers who have not yet taken that step, it is an open invitation to get involved with one of the projects in the book, or other projects in their area. Rest assured, you will be welcomed with open arms. And the harvest of all this dabbling? You'll not only get green beans, sweet peas or potatoes, but also pure happiness!

Carien van Boxtel
Garden and landscape designer
www.carienvanboxtel.com
Designer/initiator of various collectively managed gardens, including
De Toren Tuin Zaltbommel, Juliana's Hofje in Zaltbommel and Betzy's Tuun
on Vlieland.

Battery
Urban Farm

Battery Urban Farm is part of the Battery Park, located in Southern Manhattan. The Battery Urban Farm is primarily an educational farm where New York City students, residents and visitors learn more about sustainable farming techniques and can also taste new food products. The Battery Conservancy started the farm in 2011 in collaboration with the Environmental Club Millennium High School. Since then, thousands of students and volunteers have helped with harvesting many sorts of vegetables, fruits, spices, grains and flowers. The farm is partly run by a local primary school and partly by employees of the Battery Park. The primary school pupils come once a week to take care of their vegetables and their teacher also teaches them about how fruit and vegetables grow. This year, the Battery Urban farm

opened a brand new Forest Farm. Now you can walk along winding paths through a forest with mainly native plants that are edible and, or medicinal.

There are fruit trees, berry bushes, mushrooms, flowers for pollinators and specimen of medicinal plants. Through lessons in this ecosystem, students learn a lot about native plants and their pollinators , but also about how tasty fresh blueberries are. The products that are grown on the Urban Farm and the Urban Forest Farm are donated to the participating schools and to the School Café Program. During summer, food is also donated to the community partner, Drive Change, for use in their Snowday food truck.

The Battery Urban Farm is the first urban farm since the Dutch had their cotton plantations in New Amsterdam in 1625. Moreover, it is the only public farm in the lower part of Manhattan.

www.thebattery.org/projects/battery-urban-farm
Location: Battery Park, Manhattan, New York, NY, United States

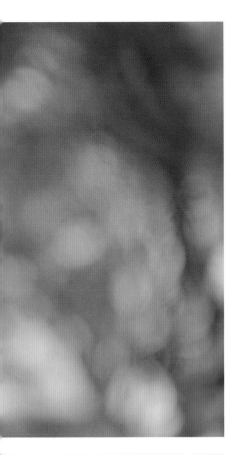

The Battery Urban Farm is the first urban farm since the Dutch had their cotton plantations in New Amsterdam in 1625.

Munthof

Munthof is a city farm on the Muntplein in Antwerp, where gardening is done organically. For decades, it was a haven for graffiti artists. Now, after a lengthy planning process, residents have reclaimed it and made it into a green neighbourhood park and communal garden.

Everyone can contribute something and learn about ecological gardening. Children from the Musica primary school have honed their vegetable gardening techniques here and are learning how to keep the five chickens: Ocher (Oker), Stripe (Streep), Speckle (Spikkel), Blackhead (Zwartkop) and White feather (Witveer). Two youth groups, Betonne Jeugd and Habbekrats, organise activities around the garden and local residents work together in it. The farm has communal planting beds and offers individual planters of one square metre for private use. Several bee hotels have been created and residents are learning how to compost. Here, in the heart of the Scheldt City in 2014, people harvested and picked courgettes, fennel, artichokes, lettuces, tomatoes, kale, red and green cabbages, cauliflower, chicory, olive cucumbers, spinach, beans, leeks, celery, various types of flowers and all kinds of herbs. To ward off unwanted visitors, the garden is enclosed, and opening hours are still to be agreed. The garden is very popular in the neighbourhood, with new people getting involved every week, including families with children, older people and creative types, who build interesting constructions. Climbing plants growing on the walls have given the square a very green aspect, making the Munthof a unique spot in the centre of Antwerp, with something for everyone.

There are now five chickens: Ocher (Oker), Stripe (Streep), Speckle (Spikkel), Blackhead (Zwartkop) and White feather (Witveer).

http://munthof.weebly.com/over-het-project.html
Location: Muntstraat, 2000 Antwerp, Belgium.

A unique spot in the
centre of Antwerp.

Salford, Greater Manchester
(United Kingdom)

The Biospheric Project

The Biospheric Project was set up inside and in front of Irwell House, a disused former printing factory on East Philip Street, Salford, Manchester. This special project includes a forest garden, a research laboratory and a retail outlet. It aims to teach urban residents about nutrition and to provide them with safe and sustainable produce.

The forest garden is located in front of the old factory. It was designed and planted with more than 30 different sorts of trees and over 50 varieties of plants. As a result, a natural forest garden arose with multiple layers of growth and mixed vegetation. Different herbs, spices, vegetables and medicinal plants grow side by side, as well as fruit and berries. The edible crops are planted in raised planters. This is because of possible contamination of the soil from the ink factory. Besides rhubarb, cabbage and fruit trees, you can also find different edible mushrooms here, grafted on tree trunks. In Irwell House itself, an inspirational agricultural laboratory researches plants, fish, chickens, worms and bees. All have found their place in a carefully constructed ecosystem that consists of a total of 78 steps. The Biospheric Project is therefore much more than an urban farm and conducts research on sustainable and robust agricultural practices in urban environments. Produce will be sold with other locally produced food in the shop, 78 Steps, named after the walking distance from the farm to the shop. From the start of the project the Salford community has been actively targeted to establish interest in sustainable urban food. Teams will soon start giving workshops, varying from cooking to permaculture, to raise awareness in local residents.

www.biosphericfoundation.com
Location: Irwell House, East Philip Street, Salford M3 7LE, United Kingdom

In Irwell House itself, an inspiring agricultural laboratory is established with plants, fish, chickens, worms and bees.

BIOSPHERIC
PROJECT

Visit our shop **78 Steps**
for fresh fruit and vegetables,
whole foods and groceries

Different herbs, spices, vegetables and medicinal plants grow side by side

Boeretuin

The **Boeretuin** is located on a piece of land in the Haarlemse Raaks, on the Boerenplein between the Jopenkerk and the former HBS-B-school.

'Boeren' means 'farmer'. Due to the economic crisis, there were no plans for this undeveloped piece of wasteland. The municipality sowed grass and planted some rose bushes. But then young people began using it as a hangout and it became little more than an ashtray and garbage dump. The late local resident Fer Daalderop thought this was a waste. He committed himself to the idea of starting an urban farm and, along with other local residents, decided this piece of land could be used in a better way. As long as there were no building plans, something beautiful could come of it.

To achieve their plan the residents asked for the help of the Haarlem Moes, a group of local people known to have green fingers. They thought about starting an organic vegetable garden, where local residents could work together and grow and eat their own food. This way everyone could profit from the garden and it would also be a meeting place. In the early spring of 2012, the residents started work on the lawn. The urban farm took shape when they installed handmade planters. Vegetables and herbs were planted with root cloth and soil, because the existing surface was not suitable for growing food. A good example was set by residents Karin van Nunen and Truus Boerma, who showed that with wood, hammer and nails, root cloth and soil, a green bin could be made in no time. Eleven small black bins were then placed in a circle and now serve as a children's playground or farm garden. Quite a few children have already planted strawberries, tomatoes and cucumber seedlings in their bins. The municipality has added eight more large planters with good soil, suitable for urban agriculture. The gardeners provide their own materials to make bins and also soil, plants and tools. In the Boeretuin people now take a great deal of pleasure from working in the gardens and sharing gardening expertise with neighbours.

www.haarlemgroener.nl
Location: Boerenplein in Haarlem, The Netherlands

Quite a few children have already put strawberries, tomatoes and cucumber herbs in their bins.

FRESH E
1egg:
1 dozen

Edgemere Farm

Edgemere Farm,
Far Rockaway, Queens, New York, is near the beach, and was struck by Hurricane Sandy in late 2012. The following spring, 596 Acres – a foundation that manages undeveloped land in New York – offered the farm some land. Local residents submitted ideas for what to do with it, and were invited to implement their plans for a vegetable and herb farm. The management of the 2,000 square metre plot was transferred to the residents.

Because of its location near the sea, the farm has poor sandy soil; so much attention is given to producing and applying compost. Residents are encouraged to hand in their organic waste. Edgemere Farm is a commercial farm, where several farmers rent a plot of land and grow their own produce. This produce, including peppers, garlic, basil and carrots, is almost all sold to local restaurants. Leftover vegetables and herbs are sold at the farmers' own local market every Saturday. Noticeable on Edgemere Farm are the many outdoor kitchens and tables, and also the solar panels used for sustainable energy. Equipment is stored in a large container, and on the roof there are beehives. A weekly dinner every Thursday during the growing season is the highlight of the week. Local chefs demonstrate their culinary skills and prepare delicious dishes using the seasonal vegetables and herbs available from the farm.

www.edgemerefarm.org
Location: 385 Beach 45th St, Far Rockaway, Queens NY 11691, United States

When you walk around on Edgemere Farm, you will notice the many outdoor kitchens and tables.

Texelhof

Buurttuin Texelhof
(Neighbourhood Garden Texelhof) is in the district of Schalkwijk in the city of Haarlem. Bart Kant, 30-something years old, had had enough of the view from his balcony, which overlooked featureless bushes. So he had the idea of creating a 50 x 10 metre organic garden for the whole neighbourhood, growing food for residents.

The original bushes belonged to a housing association, which welcomed Bart's idea, as long as other residents would back his ambitious plan. Handing out cards did not mobilise his neighbours, so Bart tried something completely different. He went from door to door and explained his plan. This generated the enthusiasm he had hoped for – almost everyone went along with the idea. The housing association gave Bart a budget, and two volunteers agreed to help. A garden centre provided free tools, and someone donated a second-hand wheelbarrow.

The tightly classified garden (De strak ingedeelde tuin) is divided into three sections. The first part is for different herbs. The vegetables, grown in a biologically dynamic way, are in the middle. They include maize, pumpkins and strawberries. One of the vegetable beds is especially designed for perennials, such as rhubarb, Jerusalem artichokes and Egyptian onions. The back of the garden will become an edible food forest, and will take some years to develop. Three years on, the neighbourhood garden is a great success. Bart works in it every day and now enjoys the views from his balcony. His neighbours are still passionate about the garden, preparing a meal together every summer using ingredients from it. Residents congregate to chat and put their organic waste on the compost heap. Thus, the garden is gradually becoming a communal one.

www.facebook.com/PermacultuurtuinTexelhof?v=timeline&filter=2
Location: Texelhof, Schalkwijk Haarlem, The Netherlands

A garden centre provided free tools and a second-hand wheelbarrow was donated as well.

The neighbourhood is still passionate about the garden.

East New York Farms

East New York Farms was established for the East Brooklyn community in 1998. It maintains several gardens as well as the main farm. The farm not only teaches youngsters how fruit and vegetables are grown, but also allows participating farmers to sell their goods at a market every Sunday. East New York Farms manages two urban farms – the UCC Youth Farm and The Hands and Heart Community Garden. They work with an ever-increasing network of gardeners. Backyards and over 60 community gardens are managed and maintained throughout Eastern New York. The mission of the East New York Farm Project is to encourage young people and adults to produce fair and healthy food. In practice, this happens by encouraging local sustainable agriculture and a community-led economy. East New York Farms is therefore a project of the United Community Centres, together with local residents. On these farms healthy and varied food is grown for the local community.

In addition, East New York Farms offers support to other groups that want to do the same. Horticulturists get support during the planning stage and help is offered when they want to take their vegetables to market. The growers produce a large number of best sellers: crispy kale and specialities from the Caribbean and South Asia (callao, bora, karela and coriander), fresh herbs and much more.

City gardens in East New York produce more than 7,000 kilograms of healthy food every year. These fruits and vegetables are free to members of the community and available for reasonable prices at the farmers' markets.

www.eastnewyorkfarms.org
Location: 613 New Lots Ave, Brooklyn, NY 11207, United States

City gardens in East
New York produce
more than seven
thousand kilograms of
healthy food every year.

Eagle Street Rooftop Farm

Eagle Street Rooftop Farm is on the roof of a large warehouse on the East River in northwest Brooklyn. It is one of the few places in New York where lettuce beds can be seen against the background of the Manhattan skyline. It has a mixed harvest of biological vegetables and there's even room for a colony of Italian bees. The market – which is open to the public on Sundays – sells freshly picked vegetables and gives people the opportunity to learn about the process of organic farming in an urban environment.

Annie Novak and Ben Flanner planted the first seeds in Eagle Street in April 2010. Since then the company has become an exemplar for the urban agriculture programme. Their farm also works with a small Community Supported Agriculture programme (CSA). Additionally Rooftop Farms takes part in Growing Chefs (Food education from the soil to the kitchen). Novak and Planner want to promote their vision and business by educating the public

and offering free workshops. Topics include: bees and beekeeping, fertilising in the city and growing vegetables. Every Sunday Eagle Street Rooftop Farm is open for anyone who is interested in voluntary work and who wants to learn more about managing an urban farm from sowing to harvesting. Goode Green originally designed the roof, and installed both the basic system and the growth medium. The farm uses a mixture of compost, fragments of rock and shale (rock composed of clay materials). The combined materials are light in weight, providing good air circulation and water transmission. A secondary benefit is that the system keeps the warehouse below cool.

http://rooftopfarms.org
Location: 44 Eagle St, Brooklyn, NY 11222, United States

The Eagle Street Rooftop is one of the few places in New York where you can see lettuce beds against the background of the Manhattan skyline!

Feedback Farms

Brooklyn's **Feedback Farms** use temporarily vacant sites for research into new methods of urban agriculture in New York City. They have had to move several times, so to make things easier they use dump sacks – known as Super Sacks – for growing vegetables and fruit. These Super Sacks are normally used for transporting heavy stone and building materials, but also make perfect, portable urban farming planters.

On a frosty winter's day in January, a software programmer called Tom Hallaran was walking on the wasteland close to his apartment. Hallaran had always been fascinated by farming and saw the possibilities of doing some bionic (technological) gardening. Three months later Hallaran, together with colleagues Clare Sullivan, Kallie Weinkle and Gregory Sogorka, established an urban farm, known as Feedback Farms. Here urban agriculture is supported by technological experiments, with plant sensors next to the tomatoes and kale. The sensors transmit information about – for example – the condition of the soil to a specially designed dashboard on Hallaran's laptop. This allows techno-farmers to check from a distance how their crops are doing. A test set shows what the produce and quality of the crop will be. By using this technology Hallaran and his team want to transform the unused sites of NYC into productive areas that can supplement food shortages in neighbourhoods.

The aim is to create farms of which communities can be proud. "We do this because we love it" is a favourite expression of Hallaran's. He wants everybody in the neighbourhood to experience his passion for urban gardening and to understand where their food comes from.

www.feedbackfarms.com
Location: 346 Bergen St, Brooklyn, NY 11217, United States

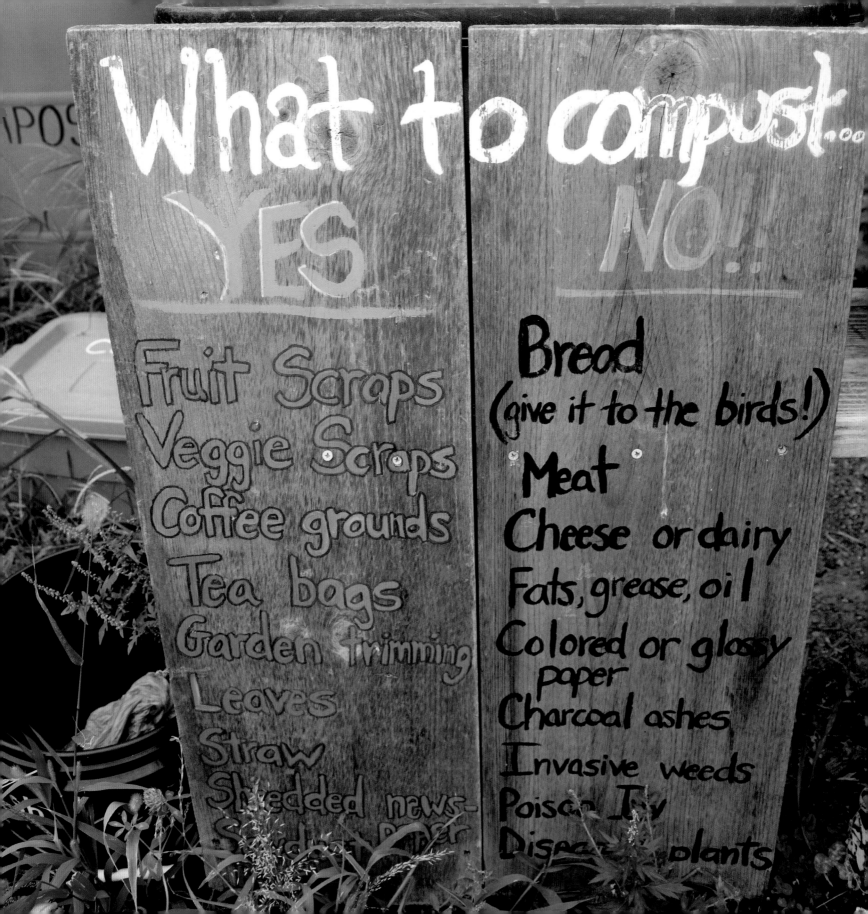

What to compost...

YES

Fruit Scraps
Veggie Scraps
Coffee grounds
Tea bags
Garden trimming
Leaves
Straw
Shredded news-
paper

NO!!

Bread
(give it to the birds!)
Meat
Cheese or dairy
Fats, grease, oil
Colored or glossy
paper
Charcoal ashes
Invasive weeds
Poison Ivy
Diseased plants

These Super Sacks are normally used for transporting heavy stone and building materials but are also applicable as planters in Urban farming.

The 462 Halsey community garden

In 2011 local Brooklyn residents founded the **462 Halsey Community Garden**. Initially, each had their own private gardens and did general maintenance as a team. But in 2013 the residents decided to turn it into a community garden so everyone from the neighbourhood could get involved. Everyone is welcome to enjoy the community garden in his or her own way. It is possible to help with the various activities in the garden, but people can also just relax in the shade of the pavilion after work and enjoy a barbecue. For the children, the community garden is a great place to play, to learn how to grow food, to get their hands dirty and to come into contact with nature. Schoolchildren are taught about different plants and how to make compost. Parties, concerts and art workshops are being organised.

The garden is decorated with wooden planters in which different kinds of vegetables and herbs flourish. The proceeds are sold on Saturday – harvest day. For only10 dollars customers can buy a box full of vegetables and herbs. The community garden is a non-profit project – volunteers do everything. The money they earn during harvest day is used for the benefit of the garden. Residents bring fruit, vegetable and garden waste for composting to fertilize the garden – nearly 20 tons since it opened in 2012. In summer, the community garden organises the Fresh Food Box programme, providing low-cost, local and healthy food for approximately 75 households per week.

To ensure the survival of the community garden, various organisations in New York have offered support.

http://462halsey.com/
Location: Halsey St, Brooklyn, NY 11233, United States

74

Since the opening of the community garden in 2012, neighbours have brought nearly 20 tons of green waste to the compost heap.

New York (United States)

Hell's Kitchen Farm Project

Hell's Kitchen Farm Project is on the roof of the Metro Baptist Church in the Hell's Kitchen district of Manhattan. This district, in the western part of Manhattan between 34th and 57th Street, is swamped with places to eat. But between the dollar pizza stands and the high-end restaurants it was hardly possible to get any healthy food. In 2014, four neighbourhood organisations decided to address this problem by constructing an urban farm on the church rooftop. One bright morning in June 2010 more than 60 volunteers were ready to start on 40th Street, and took the first steps in the transformation of the rooftop into an urban farm. That day they worked together as a bucket brigade and transferred seven tons of soil to the roof of the church in less than five hours. Once on the roof, the soil was put into more than 50 bright blue plastic children's pools. These swimming pools were planted with different types of lettuce, tomatoes, cucumbers, eggplants, potatoes and various herbs. Since early 2013,

gauze has been used to protect the vegetables and herbs from birds. The church gives away everything harvested by the volunteers through a cooperative foundation for the homeless.

The age of the church building was behind the decision to grow vegetables in plastic children's pools, in order to avoid putting too much weight on the roof. Nowadays this project is much more than an unusual looking urban farm. It has become a calm oasis in which to take a break in the middle of a hectic Manhattan. Here, people can meet friends and neighbours and come into contact with nature. Visitors to the Hell's Kitchen website often express their surprise and wonder at the presence of this Garden of Eden in Manhattan.

www.hkfp.org

Location: Metro Baptist Church Rooftop, 410 W. 40th Street, NY, United States

The old age of the church building led to the deliberate choice to grow vegetables in plastic children's pools. This way the project would not be too heavy for the roof.

The Harlem Success Garden

The Harlem Success Garden is a farm that belongs to the organisation Harlem Grown. This is a non-profit organisation with several gardens in the district of Harlem. Since 2011 Harlem Grown has developed two urban farms, several school gardens and a hydroponic greenhouse. Every year more than 1,200 children are reached as well as more than 1,000 parents, volunteers and members of the community.

Initiator Tony founded Harlem Grown in response to the obesity of many residents in his neighbourhood. Typically, there are no fewer than 50 chicken restaurants in a short radius – that's a lot of fried chicken! Children grow up in a community that has no access to the resources they need to thrive, such as a healthy diet. Harlem Grown is trying to change that pattern. Its mission is simple but clear – by involving young people in activities such as gardening, cooking and composting, they learn what a healthy lifestyle is and how to create it. But they also

learn a lot more. Under the guidance of mentors, they develop skills such as working in a team, how to resolve conflicts, being patient and dealing with responsibility. Everything they harvest is for local residents and given away for free. Any excess is sold to pay the staff.

The farm also operates as an outdoor classroom. Teachers take their classes there so children can learn about gardening. In summer there is a camp for children and movie nights are held. Since working with Harlem Grown, partner schools have noticed a drastic change in their school environments. The atmosphere and mutual relationships have strongly improved, and the various salads that include vegetables and herbs from the farm have become a favourite part of lunch.

http://harlemgrown.com
Location: 13th Street (Lennox Ave), Harlem, NY 10030, United States

SCIENCE LESSONS
IN PROGRESS
DO NOT HARVEST

Everything which
is harvested, is for
the residents in the
district and is given
away for free.

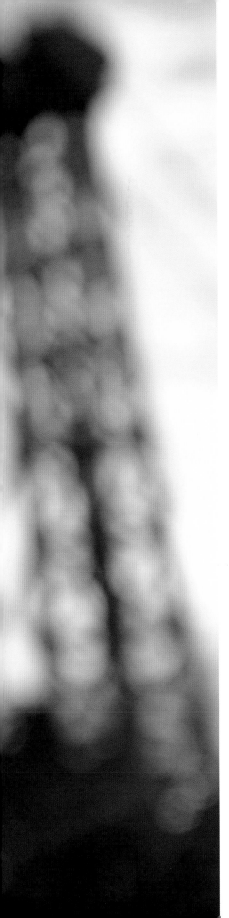

North Brooklyn Farms

In March 2013 **North Brooklyn Farms** was given access to the former parking lot of the historic Domino Sugar Refinery in Williamsburg, Brooklyn. After the refinery closed in 2004 this piece of land had been left undeveloped for nearly a decade. The founders of North Brooklyn Farms started to dig, sieve and level the land with the help of volunteers from the surrounding district. Raised beds were built with recycled scaffolding and wood from shipping pallets. The beds are portable, so the farm can be moved elsewhere when the site is redeveloped. During the building process, neighbours noticed what was happening and asked if they could help. Of course they could! Some of those volunteers became important members of the North Brooklyn Farms team. Eight volunteers now run the farm, each with a designated role. The farm began on the east side of the Williamsburg Bridge, but moved to the north side when construction work started on the original site.

It produces dozens of different vegetables and sells them at a pick-up stand nearby, or uses them to make three-course meals for sale.

As well as fruit and vegetables, the farm grows flowers such as zinnias, cosmos, sunflowers, echinacea, cornflowers and snapdragons, which it sells to the public, or to floral designers. The farm is open to the public, so that New York residents can learn about farming and methods of growing food, which are often overlooked in cities. Many visitors are local school children, who can apply the theories they learn at school by gaining practical experience on the farm.

www.northbrooklynfarms.com
Location: 329 Kent Avenue, Brooklyn, NY 11211, United States

The farm is now run
by 8 people who
are there every week
and everyone has
his own task.

The Riverpark Farm

The Riverpark Farm

is located near an office complex in Manhattan. It came about through a partnership between the River Park restaurant and the Alexandria Centre for Life Science. River Park Farm supplies fresh produce to the adjacent River Park Restaurant, headed up by River Park chef and partner Sisha Ortúzar. The farm's first location was on 430 East 29th Street in Manhattan, between First Avenue and the East River. It made use of the wasteland around the Alexandria Centre West Tower site, where construction had been temporarily suspended due to the worldwide financial crisis of recent years. An urban farm arose, which served as an example of how local wasteland could be used economically on a temporary basis. The River Park Farm not only improves the barren land, but also encourages the community to take more control, which again benefits social development in the area. In the autumn of 2012 construction was resumed at the West Tower. Thanks to innovative methods used to build the portable farm, the team was willing and able to move the 7,000 milk crates filled with plants to the new location in less than 24 hours.

The River Park Farm was reopened at a location north of the Alexandria Centre Plaza. Here the farm has to make do with less sunlight and adjust the variety of its crops. River Park Farm still cultivates fresh produce for the River Park Restaurant and is also a unique learning tool for the community and an important location for research into urban farming.

www.riverparkfarm.com
Location: 450 E 29th Street, at the North plaza of the Alexandria Centre campus, Manhattan, New York, United States

The farm came about through a partnership between the Riverpark restaurant and the Alexandria Centre for Life Science.

The Riverpark farm not only embellishes the bare land but also encourages the community to take more initiatives which again benefits social contacts in the area.

Randall's Island Urban Farm

The farm is on Randall's Island, east of Northern Manhattan. The project has been running for seven years and is part of the Randall's Island Park. Two farmers run the project and work at the farm full-time to keep it in order. Schools often visit – students can help in the garden and learn more about gardening and healthy food. The urban farm is about half an acre in size and includes many different organically grown fruits and vegetables. With more than 80 raised planters, two greenhouses and a trellis tunnel for gourds and vines, there is quite a range of crops, breeds and cultivation techniques for visitors of all ages to admire. Besides different vegetables, there are blueberries, raspberries, cranberries, fig vines and pear and apple trees. The orchard contains 40 Newton Pippins, the original apple tree from New York City. There are also a dozen Kazakhstan apple trees – this is considered the oldest kind of apple in the world. The farm is also home to the only four rice fields in New York, where six different kinds of rice from around the world are cultivated. This staple food is beautiful and fascinating to look at.

Randall's Island Urban Farm is made possible by generous donations and support from volunteer groups. The work carried out by the volunteers varies from making picnic tables to mulching raised planters. Students and schoolchildren also volunteer regularly at the farm and perform many different tasks. The day ends with a meal that they have prepared together from the farm's produce.

http://randallsisland.org/environment/urban-farm
Location: 20 Randall's Island Park, Manhattan, NY 10035, United States

Randall's Island Urban farm is made possible by generous donations and support from volunteer groups.

The Urban Farm is about half an acre in size and includes a large variety of organically grown fruits and vegetables.

The Hague (The Netherlands)

Margarethaland

Urban farm **Margarethaland** in the neighbourhood of Mariahoeve in The Hague was opened in the spring of 2013. The idea came from a neighbours' initiative, working with the foundation De Tuinen van Mariahoeve and the housing corporation Vestia. On the lawn between some 1960s-built flats, six vegetable containers a square metre in size were erected as a trial. The project foundered because of lack of water and expertise. But one year later, ten residents restarted the project – this time in open ground. The municipality supported the project immediately by putting up a fence, tilling the ground and supplying compost. Vestia paved the paths and agreed to fill the water barrels. Audrey van der Kloor of Urban Green Projects was asked to supervise. Through all four seasons in a whole year, she was present on location to advise and help out. Working with the residents, an attractive garden plan was developed. The vegetable garden now covers 200 square metres spread over 16 plots. The residents can – and do – decide for themselves what they want to grow.

"You will find a large variety of vegetables here, such as carrots, green beans, zucchinis, eggplants, garlic, tomatoes, Turkish peppers, chard and lettuce – and delicious sweet strawberries," Audrey says. "In addition, there are also all kinds of herbs: parsley, coriander, thyme, rosemary, chives and basil, to name just a few."

In particular, Moroccan mint is often used to make delicious fresh mint tea. In a separate border you can find bee-attracting flowers, colourful annual flowering shrubs and a few beautiful buddleia (butterfly bushes) to attract butterflies. Now, about 15 residents participate in the project, with eight of them actively involved on a day-to-day basis. Various activities are organised around the vegetable garden, such as a neighbourhood party at harvest time with soup and other dishes made from the garden's vegetables.

www.facebook.com/urbangreenprojects
Location: Margarethaland, district Mariahoeve, The Hague, The Netherlands

"You will find a large variety of vegetables here, such as carrots, green beans, zucchinis, eggplants, garlic, tomatoes, Turkish peppers, chard and lettuce.

Together with the residents an attractive garden plan was developed. The vegetable garden now covers two hundred square metres, spread over sixteen garden plots.

M2

HOT PEPPERS!
'Long Thin Cayenne'

The Youth Farm

THE YOUTH FARM MARKET
every wed.
june 25 -oct 29

WE ACCEPT EBT, WIC, HEALTH BUCKS, SENIOR COUPONS!

The headmaster at the High School for Public Service in Brooklyn established the Youth Farm – a unique urban farm at the entrance to the school in the heart of Brooklyn. Students mostly run the farm, growing affordable organic vegetables, flowers and herbs over 4,000 square metres for the Wingate community and its neighbours. They grow more than 80 kinds and varieties of food crops and over 60 kinds of cut flowers. Using sustainable farming methods, the Youth Farm shuns artificial pesticides and genetically modified seeds. The students sell their products through a Community Supported Agriculture (CSA) programme and a weekly farmer's market every Wednesday afternoon until the end of October. Here it is possible to buy fresh local produce and flowers and to sample healthy snacks provided by the students in cookery demonstrations.

The Youth Farm supplies several restaurants in Brooklyn. It also offers New Yorkers the opportunity to increase their knowledge about the food system and teaches them the skills they need to grow organic food themselves or with their neighbours. Once a month the Youth Farm offers free workshops on gardening and lectures on various nutrition topics. The topics may vary from sowing plants to the benefits of healthy food.

http://hspsfarm.blogspot.com
Location: 600 Kingston Ave Brooklyn, NY 11203, United States

On approximately four thousand square metres
organic and affordable vegetables, herbs and
flowers are grown for the Wingate community
and its neighbours.

Gent (Belgium)

Dakmoestuin

The **Dakmoestuin** (Rooftop Kitchen Garden) was created in 2015 on Labour Day. This was not a complete coincidence, because no less than ten cubic metres of soil had to be brought onto the roof of Galveston, an old textile factory in Gent. The first Belgian rooftop kitchen garden by Roof Food was built on the roof of Gaston, a rooftop restaurant in Gent. The Rooftop Kitchen Garden is an experimental garden of 50 square metres. In 2016 a rooftop kitchen garden of 500 square metres will be created on the roof of a business centre, where Roof Food will also have its own kitchen. The experimental garden is a chance to gain experience that can be used in the move to the new site. When Roof Food constructed the original kitchen garden they used a special roof garden substrate, rather than ordinary garden soil. This is a mixture of compost, lava rock, pumice, peat and coir. About 15 volunteers were there to carry the bags up to the roof and fill 1x5 metre wooden kitchen garden bins. In these wooden bins herbs are cultivated that are used in so-called 'roof dishes'. There are also plants such as lettuce, pole beans, cucumbers and zucchinis, which will be used later in the summer when the group organises workshops.

Sabien Windels, the inspiration behind Roof Food, brought the kitchen garden into the parts of the city where there is plenty of space and lots of sunshine – on the rooftops. By attending workshops, residents will get an understanding of gardening and cooking to the rhythm of the seasons, as well as enjoying a great view. Besides workshops, Roof Food will also provide the city's workers with a fresh dish or bowl of soup every day. A bike messenger or natural gas car will deliver daily to offices. The ingredients for these meals will be picked daily by Roof Food's cook from the rooftop garden, supplemented by organic goods from other local producers.

www.rooffood.be
Location: Wiedauwkaai 52, Gent, Belgium

The Rooftop kitchen garden is an experimental garden of fifty square metres.

About fifteen volunteers were there to carry the bags up to the roof and divide them into the wooden kitchen garden bins of 1x5 m.

Gent (Belgium)

The Site

Regularly Turkish women organise a barbeque, with halal meat so everyone can eat.

The Site is situated in the centre of the Gent neighbourhood Rabot-Blaisantvest. In 2006 the factory buildings of Alcatel Bell in the Gasmeterlaan were demolished, and a very large area became available. The city and Tondelier Development Company together wanted to renovate the area into a sustainable residential neighbourhood with a sports hall, nursery, youth centres and park. Because this would take years to develop, the large concrete factory floor was to remain unused for the time being.

At the end of 2006, local residents, the Rocsa, Community Development Gent Association and the City of Gent joined forces. Soon three projects were launched on what was now known as The Site, sponsored by municipal subsidy from Wijk aan Zet. These were 80 allotment gardens, an outdoor cinema and a traffic park. The Site houses 160 mini vegetable gardens of 4 square metres each, and a conservatory. Planters, covered with paving stones, have been built on the old factory floor. Residents can rent a plot and use common working materials, or attend a workshop organised by Velt. On top of the former factory floor two city fields have been created.

Approximately 4,000 sandbags contain 3,000 cubic metres of black gold – soil that provides 3,000 square metres of fertility. Chickens provide both a lively presence and lots of fresh eggs, which quickly find their way to volunteers and the Social Grocery. Since 2012 The Site has even had its very own beehives. The bees provide additional activity and their own Rabot-honey. Different cultures interact on The Site. Everyone takes good care of the allotment gardens and gets on well. Residents learn from each other and share tips about sowing and planting, and help each other with gardening jobs. Turkish women regularly organise a barbeque, with halal meat, so everyone can eat together. The vegetables and herbs grown on The Site go to the Social Grocery, Eatery Toreke and local residents. In this way, The Site advocates the short chain principle where vegetables and grown and eaten in the neighbourhood without causing pollution, using energy-consuming refrigerators or needing transport. And everything is always fresh!

www.rabotsite.be/en
Location: Gasmeterlaan Gent, Belgium

The Site houses one hundred and sixty mini vegetable gardens of 4 square metres each and a conservatory.

Planters, covered with paving stones, have been built on the old factory floor.

Growing Communities

Growing Communities, in the North East London borough of Hackney, is a social enterprise run by local residents. Its target is to provide alternatives to the current food system. Allan's Garden in Hackney is one of three gardens that belong to Growing Communities, where vegetables, herbs and fruit are grown organically. It is in tucked away in Allan's Park, between flats on the corner of Bethune Road and Manor Road. It is a large piece of land with a greenhouse, a small building and an ancient wall that provides passage to the herb and fruit garden.

Food is grown by and for the community. Boxes of the harvested organic vegetables and herbs are available to subscribers. The produce is also sold through a number of shops and to restaurants. The boxes offer a wide variety of fresh produce during the greater part of the year. Organic farming is better for soil, for nature and for people, so no harmful chemicals are used. Instead, plants, soil and troublesome pests are managed through techniques such

as mulching, combining plants and crop rotation. Volunteers help make Hackney salads and other products from Hackney urban farm produce. Monday is volunteers' day in Allan's Gardens.

Growing Communities also provides training for volunteers and classes for school children. Special educational programmes have been developed and explanatory signs educate visitors about what they see in the garden. In this way younger generations will come to know nature and understand how different sorts of vegetables and fruit in Allan's Garden are grown and developed.

www.growingcommunities.org
Location: The Old Fire Station, 61 Leswin Road, London N16 7NX, United Kingdom

Tucked away in Allan's Park, between flats on the corner of Bethune Road and Manor Road, you can find the Urban farm 'Allan's Garden'.

Perennials

Our main focus on these sites is salad leaves but you'll also see other food plants around our gardens. Perennials are plants that live longer than two years.

We grow blackcurrants, strawberries and lots of herbs as well as asparagus, rhubarb, herbs and fruit trees. These give us a small harvest every year and bring extra interest to the site.

Another use for plants growing on allotment sites. Did you know that some attract butterflies? They also provide an early source of nectar. Ladybirds eat the aphids which damage our crops. The flowers attract them on to eat the aphids.

Everything on our allotment is grown using organic methods. This means we grow our plants without the use of chemicals.

There are signs which explain what you can see,
so attention is paid to education as well. Food is
grown by and for the community.

148

Goosefoot family *Chenopodiaceae*

This is the third year of the rotation. The vegetables in this family can all be recognised by the shape of their leaves, which look like a goose's foot. We grow spinach, leaf beet and rainbow chard, which has a prettier, coloured stalks, and red orache, which is a novelty different coloured leaves can be eaten young and fresh in our salads, or if you let them grow big, they can be cooked as a healthy green vegetable.

You might sometimes see other plants growing next to the salads and vegetables. This is called companion planting - like flowers and the pot Marigold Calendula attract predatory insects, which then prey on other insects that want to eat our vegetables.

We use the flowers in our salad bags - another sign that they are super fresh, since flowers don't transport too well you won't see them in salad from the supermarket.

The organic vegetables and herbs which are harvested are available in the so-called Growing-Community box which you can subscribe to.

Growing Communities also provides training for volunteers and classes for school children.

Mobiele
moestuin

The **Mobiele moestuin (Mobile Kitchen Garden)** is a project created by Lonneke Rhodens, board member of Slow Food Haarlem, in the former Ripperda barracks in Haarlem. A redevelopment plan had been created for the area and partially implemented, but the final phase was delayed by the financial crisis. This had left an area of 5,000 square meters uncultivated for two years. Lonneke thought it would be a waste to do nothing with it and came up with the idea of the mobile kitchen garden. Her idea won the City Challenge prize and within a short period of time the garden became a reality.

Lonneke's idea was actually quite simple – an undeveloped piece of land would temporarily be cultivated into a lively kitchen garden by and for the local residents, until it was ultimately built on. Lonneke started with the piece of land in the Ripperdastraat. Once dug out, a beautiful piece of land emerged that the residents wanted to work on. As a result, 70 families now each have a garden of 10 square metres. They enthusiastically roll up their sleeves and grow different kinds of vegetables, herbs and flowers. It was agreed with the City of Haarlem that once the original construction plans were be implemented, Lonneke would look for a new location. The 70 families rent a piece of kitchen garden for 20 euros a year. For children there are square metre planters, in which they learn to grow vegetables. The space involves more than just gardening. While hoeing and scrabbling in the garden, rediscovering the origins of food and above all enjoying the delicious fresh vegetables and herbs, the social contacts among the residents have increased. "This form of urban agriculture is getting somewhere and the idea appears to be quite flexible," enthuses Lonneke. "People are occupied, they meet other people and have access to fresh food."

www.groendichterbij.nl/mobielemoestuin

Location: Ritmeesterstraat, Ripperda area, Haarlem, The Netherlands

For children there are the so-called square metres planters which they learn to grow vegetables

People are occupied,
they meet other people
and have access to
fresh food.

Rotterdamse Munt

After plans for a housing project were put aside, a piece of wasteland along the Rotterdam Laan van Zuid lay idle until 2013. Ingrid Ackermans and Guido Zeck of the Rotterdam-based design agency Botersloot thought it a shame to leave the area unused. They established the Rotterdam Munt foundation, and within a short period of time a green area arose at the southern entrance of the Kop van Zuid.

"There are so few green meeting spaces in urban areas, so what could be better than to put one here?" says Ingrid.

Everyone is welcome at the city nursery garden and the space is easy to maintain. In addition to growing and harvesting mint and several other herbs, the herb nursery is primarily a work experience project. Moroccan, Turkish and Surinamese women from surrounding neighbourhoods such as Afrikaanderwijk, Hillesluis, Bloemhof and Feijenoord, as well as women from other cultures, come to grow herbs and mint plants here. Many know all about the cultivation and use of herbs because of their backgrounds. Local businesses, such as groceries and catering companies, buy the organic mint, and special herbs can be grown on request. Non-trade customers can also buy herbs and herby products, such as spicy pastes and snacks. Also available are mint lemonade and, of course, mint tea. The city nursery garden is made from raised plant beds, filled with different herbs and enclosed by a green fence. Nowadays, the herb garden grows more than 100 different herb varieties, including many of Mediterranean origin. In the urban climate these herbs thrive when put in the right soil and given proper care.

www.rotterdamsemunt.nl
Location: Laan op Zuid. Entrance at de Brede Hilledijk 2 or Hilledijk 56, 3072 KG Rotterdam, The Netherlands

At the request of chefs
several special herbs
can be grown.

Everyone is welcome
in the city nursery
garden and the work
is easy.

Moroccan, Turkish and Surinamese women as well as women from other cultures grow herbs and mint plants at this site.

Het
Seinwezen

Het Seinwezen is a beautiful former Dutch Railways building beside the Haarlem railway. Next to it, residents of the Garenkokerskwartier district have been gardening since 2013. They are passionate about cultivating vegetables, herbs, fruit and flowers in 50 planters made from converted pallets, randomly scattered on either side of the track. An abandoned locomotive and wagon on the track provide an interesting backdrop. The land belongs to Dutch Railways and Prorail, and both parties have given their consent to the neighbourhood vegetable garden.

Sustainability is very important to Het Seinwezen, and it was the community's immediate wish to give the surrounding area a green future. In 2012 a group of activists began to develop the garden. An important consideration was that the soil could be contaminated, as the area had been the site of a cotton factory in the past. This was the reason for using mobile planters.

In the autumn of 2012, the residents collected pallets that had been discarded after maintenance work in the neighbourhood. On a very cold winter Sunday, with a wind chill factor of -12 degrees C, 11 men and women converted 100 pallets into 50 vegetable planters, each about one metre square. They covered them with root-resistant fabric and filled them with organic garden soil. Now residents who want to grow their own vegetables, flowers, fruit and herbs manage them individually. Many people have got to know each other because of Het Seinwezen, and together they are ensuring a green future for the neighbourhood.

www.seinwezen.nl/nieuws/zaaiwezen-buurtmoestuin-bij-het-seinwezen
Location: Kinderhuissingel 1, 2013 AS Haarlem, The Netherlands

These vegetable planters, each about one square metre, are covered with anti-root fabric and filled with organic garden soil.

Torentuin

The **Toren Tuin (Tower Garden)** in Zaltbommel is a green public hangout for people of all ages and has something for everyone to enjoy. Prior to the garden's creation, the 1.5 hectares of wasteland had become an eyesore, covered with dog waste and other rubbish. Once, a convent had stood here. More recently it was the site of a retirement home. The latter had been demolished to make way for 60 apartments, but due to the economic crisis only 20 of these were finished by 2011.

Residents decided they had put up with it for long enough. The municipality and housing association wanted to turn it into a grass field the size of one and a half football pitches, but residents believed this was asking for trouble – and certainly inviting more dog mess. They got together to form a plan, using a spatial design by Arjan Nienhuis and Carien van Boxtel. Shell paths were installed, and the vegetable and flower gardens were cultivated and planted.

Eventually, this wonderful green hangout – made by residents, for residents – emerged. The garden includes a vegetable garden with special crops, lots of green space and a natural playground with water and a hand pump, so children can learn about what grows, what flourishes… and what quacks. There is also a place where children can plant their own gardens, a playground where they can kick a ball, a lot of ornamental flowers and flowers for picking, a herb garden, an orchard with standard native trees, an apiary and a flower meadow.

Between these there are footpaths and benches where people can take in the view. There is a lawn with flowers and a natural playground with lots of wooden climbing objects. In the autumn of 2013 a fruit orchard was planted, with trees sponsored by various individuals and companies. At last the place has a soul.

There are regular work mornings to plant and maintain the garden, to work on the natural playground and for school classes and others to be shown around or given the chance to participate.

The Tower Garden is in constant use as a venue for various events and activities. Meanwhile, a beekeeper has found a permanent home here. In 2014 the Tower Garden won the Icon Project award Groen Dichterbij (Bringing nature closer to people) in the province of Gelderland, crowning the collaborative work that has led to this special city garden.

http://groendichterbij.nl/torentuinzaltbommel
Location: Vogelenzang/Agnietenstraat, near the church square, Zaltbommel, The Netherlands.

DE TORENTUIN

There is a lawn with flowers and a natural playground with lots of wooden climbing objects was created.

Meanwhile, a beekeeper has found a permanent place in The Tower Garden.

Tuin op de Pier

The **Tuin op de Pier (Garden on the Pier)** is located on the Lloyd Pier, Delfshaven, Rotterdam, between the old harbour and the Nieuwe Maas. The pier is named after Rotterdam Lloyd, a shipping company that was based here. Construction of residential complexes is almost finished here, but due to the financial crisis a large area intended for apartment buildings has never been developed. The wasteland was polluted, unattractive and deplored by local people. Finally, fed up with having to look at it, residents submitted a proposal to the municipality to create a temporary park. They received permission and united in a foundation. This group of volunteers now temporarily administrates more than 9,000 square metres of land. The remaining 1,000 square metres of wasteland has become a large field in which to play, rest and picnic, surrounded by bee-friendly wild flowers to pick.

More than 100 residents of the Lloyd Pier are now involved. The huge piece of land on Garden Pier is divided into three areas:

an orchard with 13 fruit trees, the field where dogs are allowed to play and a vegetable garden. None of the houses have gardens and their balconies are not favourable for growing, as they do not have sunlight. The residents all enjoy having this green space in their neighbourhood. Regular gatherings are organised, such as a harvest home, a rabbit or kale meal and a weeding-pizza- relay race. There are also workshops on digging, pruning and preserving vegetables. These activities encourage neighbourliness. The garden attracts many visitors, including both local residents and people who live elsewhere.

www.tuinopdepier.nl
Location: Lloydkade, 3024 Rotterdam, The Netherlands

There are workshops on digging, pruning and preserving vegetables. These activities encourage neighbourliness.

188

The residents of
the Lloyd District
united themselves
in a foundation with
a large group of
volunteers.

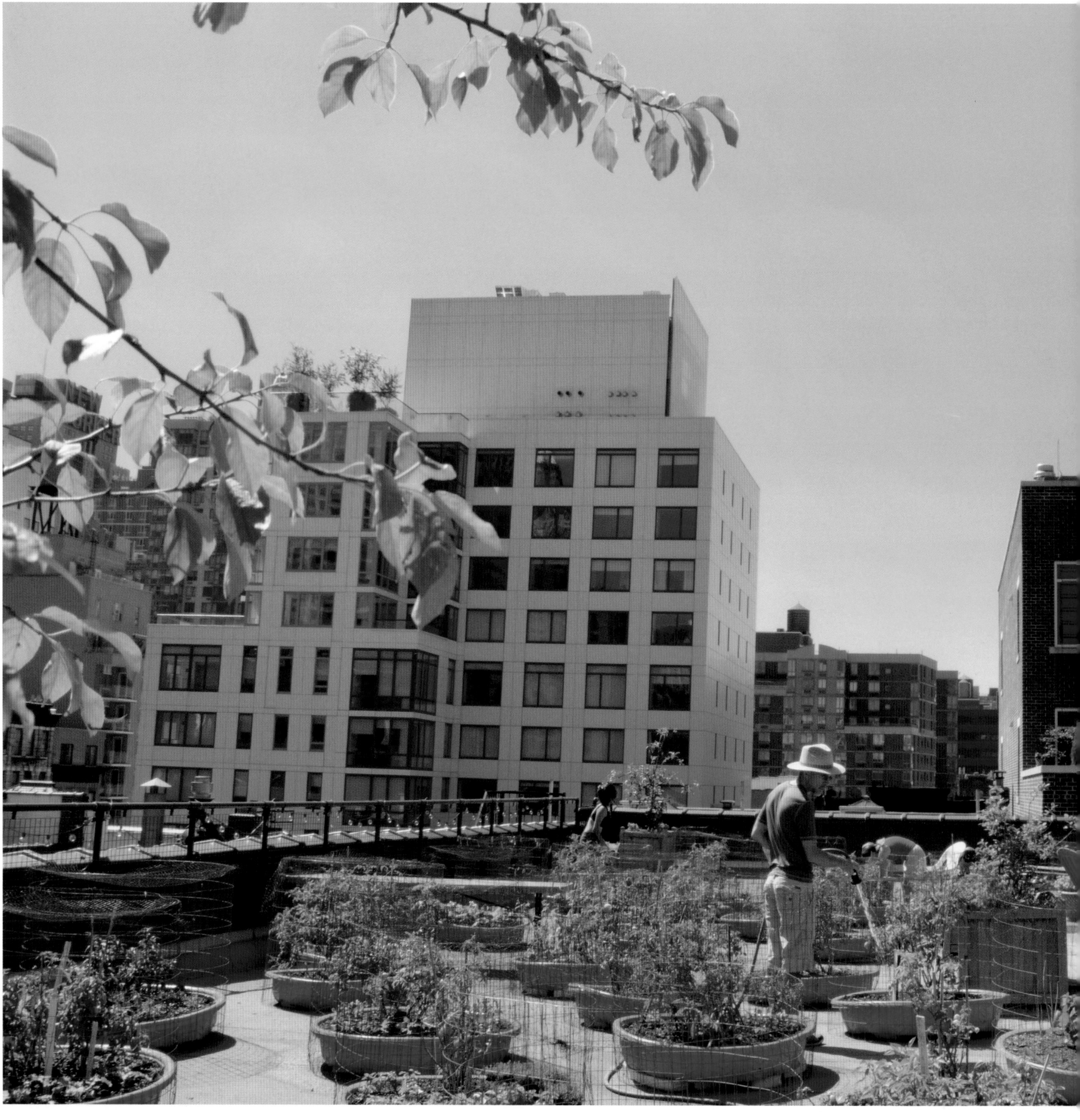

Nuno Clauzing was born in Gouda, The Netherlands and studied Tourism after his secondary education. Ever since he was a child, he has had a passion for travelling and photography, just like his father. In 2014 Nuno started his own company, Nuno Clauzing Photography. Nuno is strongly attracted by The United States of America and captured New York for this book. The past few years he has travelled through America a number of times and has enjoyed its diversity, the skylines of its cities and its beautiful nature.

Hans Clauzing grew up in Voorburg, The Netherlands, with an interest in photography and nature. He went to the forestry technical school with the idea of becoming a forester. But his interests changed and Hans came into contact with the floriculture sector. He studied floriculture and trees cultivation for three years after which he trained as a teacher of biology and home economics. In 1995 he took the plunge and decided to combine his hobbies, photography and gardens, into his work. Meanwhile Hans writes and takes photographs for various international gardening magazines.

We would like to thank everybody who inspired us, welcomed us at the gardens and contributed in any way to the creation of this book.